BUTTERFLIES

Published by Creative Education, Inc., 123 South Broad Street, Mankato, Minnesota 56001

Printed by permission of Wildlife Education, Ltd.

Library of Congress Cataloging-in-Publication Data

Biel, Timothy L.
Butterflies / by Timothy Levi Biel.
p.   cm. — (Zoobooks)
Summary: Discusses butterflies, their metamorphosis, and their migration and presents some butterfly-related activities.
ISBN 0-88682-421-4
1. Butterflies—Juvenile literature. [1. Butterflies.] I. Title. II. Series: Zoo books (Mankato, Minn.)
QL544.2.B54   1991   599.78'9—dc20   91-9829 CIP AC

BUTTERFLIES

Series Created by
John Bonnett Wexo

Written by
Beth Wagner Brust

Zoological Consultant
Charles R. Schroeder, D.V.M.
Director Emeritus
San Diego Zoo &
San Diego Wild Animal Park

Scientific Consultants
Dan Lindsley, Ph.D.
Bob Brock
Zoological Society of San Diego

Creative Education

Art Credits

Pages Eight and Nine: Davis Meltzer; **Pages Ten and Eleven:** Chuck Ripper; **Pages Twelve and Thirteen:** Davis Meltzer; **Pages Sixteen and Seventeen:** Chuck Ripper; **Pages Eighteen and Nineteen:** Davis Meltzer; **Pages Twenty and Twenty-one:** Davis Meltzer; **Activities Art:** Elizabeth Morales-Denney.

Photographic Credits

Front Cover: John Cancalosi (DRK Photo); **Pages Six and Seven:** Pat and Tom Leeson (Photo Researchers, Inc.); **Page Ten: Upper Right,** L. West (Bruce Coleman, Inc.); **Middle Left,** L. West (Photo Researchers, Inc.); **Page Eleven: Upper Left,** Alice K. Taylor (Photo Researchers, Inc.); **Lower Right,** Cristina Smith (Wildlife Education, Ltd.); **Page Twelve:** Alfred Pasieka (Bruce Coleman, Ltd.); **Page Thirteen:** Raymond A. Mendez (Animals Animals); **Pages Fourteen and Fifteen:** Michael Fogden (DRK Photo); **Page Sixteen: Middle Left,** Alan Blank (Bruce Coleman, Inc.); **Lower Left,** Anthony Bannister (NHPA); **Page Seventeen:** M. Chinery (Natural Science Photos); **Page Nineteen: Upper Right,** Gregory G. Dimijian, M.D. (Photo Researchers, Inc.); **Middle Right,** Jeff Foott (Survival Anglia); **Lower Right,** Frans Lantingh (Bruce Coleman, Ltd.); **Page Twenty:** Stanley Breeden (DRK Photo); **Page Twenty-one: Upper Right,** Steven L. Hilty (Bruce Coleman, Inc.); **Middle Right,** Frans Lanting (Minden Pictures); **Page Twenty-two, Upper Left,** Stephen Dalton/Oxford Scientific Films (Animals Animals); **Lower Left and Bottom,** Marty Knapp (Wildlife Education, Ltd.).

Our Thanks To: Mark Scriber, Ph.D. (Michigan State University); Gordon Gordh, Ph.D. (University of California, Riverside); Charles Hogue, Ph.D. and Brian Harris (Los Angeles County Museum of Natural History); John Rollins (Carnegie Museum); Sam Johnson (Field Museum of Natural History); Linda Coates and Valerie Hare (San Diego Zoo Library); Jean Lindsley; Sean Brust; Paul Brust; Joe Selig.

Contents

Butterflies play an important role in our world. Everyone knows how beautiful butterflies can be. But many people do not realize that they do much more than simply make the world a prettier place.

For one thing, butterflies carry pollen from plant to plant. This helps fruits, vegetables, and flowers to produce new seeds, which in turn become new plants. Also, butterflies—as well as caterpillars—are at the bottom of the food chain. This means that they provide food for many other types of animals.

The word "butterfly" was probably first used to describe a common European butterfly, the yellow Brimstone. At first, people called it the "butter-colored fly." Then the word was shortened to "butterfly."

Scientists group butterflies along with moths into the category called *Lepidoptera* (lep-uh-DOP-turr-uh), which means "scaled wings." This name fits butterflies and moths very well since their wings and bodies are covered with tiny scales. In fact, they are the only insects that have scales.

Butterflies can be found in all but the very hottest and coldest parts of the world. More butterflies live in the tropics than anywhere else. That's because in the tropics, there are always plenty of plants for them to feed on. Tropical butterflies also live the longest—some for up to 1 year! Butterflies that live in more temperate climates have an average lifespan of just a few weeks or, at most, two months.

People have always been fascinated by butterflies. In the 1800s, butterfly collecting enjoyed great popularity. People would hunt, collect, and study whatever specimens they could find. But these days, with so many excellent cameras available, some butterfly lovers are photographing butterflies rather than catching them.

Another way people have discovered that they can get close to butterflies is by making a special garden. By planting certain flowers and grasses, butterfly watchers can attract butterflies from their region. What better place to watch butterflies than in your own backyard!

Western Tiger Swallowtail Butterfly

Twenty thousand species of butterflies brighten the world. As you can see, butterflies have a wonderful variety of colors, wing shapes, and sizes. The largest is the *Queen Alexandra Birdwing.* It has a bigger wingspan than many birds. The world's smallest butterfly, the *Small Blue,* measures less than an inch from wingtip to wingtip.

No two butterflies are exactly alike. Even two members of the same species are always a bit different. Often, the most colorful butterflies are males. Females tend to be duller looking, so that they can blend in with their surroundings. This helps protect them from predators while laying their eggs. But whether male or female, large or small, butterflies make fields, forests, and mountainsides come alive when they flutter and soar through the air!

CRACKER BUTTERFLY
Hamadryas chloe
(South and Central America)

NORTH AMERICAN TIGER SWALLOWTAIL
Papilio glaucus
(North America)

GOLD-SPOT SKIPPER
Aguna asander
(North America)

CABBAGE BUTTERFLY
Artogeia rapae
(North America)

PEACOCK BUTTERFLY
Inachis io
(Europe)

TREE NYMPH
Idea leuconoe
(Southeast Asia)

QUEEN ALEXANDRA BIRDWING (MALE)
Ornithoptera alexandrae
(New Guinea)

DOG FACE BUTTERFLY
Zerene cesonia
(Southwestern United States)

COMMON BLUEBOTTLE
Graphium sarpedon
(Australia to India)

AUSTRALIAN REGENT SKIPPER
Euschemon rafflesia
(Australia)

PAINTED LADY
Vanessa cardui
(North and South America, Europe, Africa, Asia, and Australia)

GREAT NORTHERN SULPHER
Colias gigantea
(Arctic North America)

BLOOD-RED CYMOTHOE
Cymothoe sangaris
(Africa)

CITRUS SWALLOWTAIL
Papilio demodocus
(Africa)

QUEEN ALEXANDRA BIRDWING (FEMALE)
Ornithoptera alexandrae
(New Guinea)

The largest butterfly in the world is the female *Queen Alexandra Birdwing*, with a wingspan of 11 inches (28 centimeters). The world's smallest butterfly is probably the *Small Blue*. It is so tiny that it could fit on the tip of your nose!

SMALL BLUE
Philotiella speciosa
(Asia and Europe)

T he way a butterfly changes from a slow, clumsy caterpillar into a beautiful, graceful adult is one of the most magical events in nature. This process, called *metamorphosis* (met-uh-MORE-fuh-siss), is not unique to butterflies. In fact, all insects go through a similar change—but none more dramatically than the butterfly.

There are four stages in a butterfly's metamorphosis. Every butterfly begins life as an *egg*. In time, a tiny *caterpillar* hatches from the egg. The caterpillar grows and eventually turns into a *chrysalis* (KRIS-uh-liss). Finally, from the chrysalis, an *adult butterfly* emerges. The entire life cycle of a butterfly usually lasts less than two months. But there are a few kinds of tropical butterflies that live up to one full year.

1 Female butterflies lay their eggs in small clusters. Since each species of caterpillar eats only the leaves of certain plants, the female must select just the right plant on which to lay her eggs.

Butterfly eggs, like the ones above, come in many shapes and textures. Some are smooth, while others have grooves on their surface.

2 After 4 or 5 days, the egg is ready to hatch. Then the caterpillar eats its way out of the egg head first.

Caterpillars live to eat. With their massive jaws, they munch on plant leaves from dusk until dawn. In their short lifetime, they may eat as much as *20 times their weight* in food.

3 Once free of the egg, the caterpillar turns and eats its shell. The eggshell provides important nutrients that the caterpillar will need to keep growing.

Before shedding its skin for the last time, the caterpillar attaches itself to a stem by spinning a silk "button." Once secure, it wriggles out of its old skin to expose a tough new skin. This new skin hardens almost immediately— it is called a *chrysalis*.

5

■ Legs
■ Head
■ Wing
■ Thorax
□ Abdome

4 A caterpillar's skin cannot stretch as it grows. So, like snakes, caterpillars must shed their skin to make room for their bigger bodies. After each shedding, they look completely different!

6 Inside the chrysalis, the caterpillar's eyes, legs, and body are broken down into a thick liquid. Slowly, the parts o the adult butterfly begin to form. Thi process may take days, weeks, or eve months. Can you make out the parts of the developing butterfly in the chrysalis above?

Once outside the chrysalis, the butterfly's crumpled wings also fill with fluid and take shape. The wings must fill quickly, or they will harden before they have reached their full size.

⟨8⟩

⟨7⟩

When the butterfly is ready to emerge, it splits open the chrysalis by pumping fluids from its abdomen into its head and upper body. It then crawls out legs first, and turns around to cling to its shell. Its crumpled wings hang downward so that they can unfold more easily.

⟨9⟩

It usually takes a couple of hours for the butterfly's wings to dry and harden in their correct shape. Then it can fly away in search of its first meal.

Imagine what it would be like to be a caterpillar turning into a beautiful butterfly. Find a colorful towel. Put it under a blanket or inside a sleeping bag. Then pretend you're a caterpillar and slowly crawl under the blanket or into the bag. Curl up inside so that it's very dark and snug.

Now wiggle around in the dark and find two corners of the towel. Once you've grabbed them, jump out as the winged wonder — now you're *Super Butterfly*!

*E*very butterfly is covered with millions of tiny scales—from the tip of its wings to the bottom of its feet. Scales have many uses. They help control body temperature. And because they rub off easily, they help the butterfly escape the grip of predators.

Scales also give butterflies their beautiful colors. These colors serve many purposes. They may be used to attract mates. They may be used to warn predators that a butterfly is poisonous. Or they may help a butterfly blend in with its surroundings.

A butterfly's body is divided into three sections. Like all insects, it has a *head*, a *thorax* (THORE-acks), and an *abdomen* (AB-doe-mun). Like most flying insects, butterflies have six legs, four wings, and two antennae. But butterflies have a special grace and beauty that is all their own.

Here is a close-up view of a butterfly's scales. You can see how they overlap like shingles on a roof. Underneath the scales, butterfly wings are clear and thin like cellophane.

• Moth antennae are pointed at the ends, not knobbed like a butterfly's.

• Most moths fly at night. Butterflies usually fly by day, although a few species fly at dusk.

The moth is the butterfly's closest relative. Here are a few simple ways to tell moths and butterflies apart.

• Most moths have fatter bodies than butterflies do. And they are usually much less colorful.

A butterfly's skeleton is on the *outside* of its body, instead of on the inside like yours. It is called an *exoskeleton* (EX-oh-skel-uh-tun). It provides the insect with a hard, protective covering for its soft insides.

As incredible as it sounds, a butterfly *tastes with its feet!* As soon as it lands on a flower, it uses its feet, called *tarsi* (TAR-see), to tell whether this is the flower it wants. If you tasted your food the way a butterfly does, you would have to put your toes in your dessert to sample it!

URVILLIANUS BIRDWING

Have you ever seen a butterfly resting on the ground with its wings wide open? It's soaking up the sun's heat. Butterflies need to warm their muscles in the sunshine before they can fly away.

Although butterflies cannot fly as fast as birds, they use their wings in the same way to flutter, glide, and soar. Some butterflies beat their wings *as many as 40 times per second!* And their top flying speed is more than 16 miles per hour (26 kilometers per hour)—that's amazing for such a small animal!

Butterflies use their antennae as feelers to *touch* things. They use them to *smell* odors in the air. And they use them to *sense* the movement of the air, which helps them get where they want to go.

To sip nectar, butterflies have a long hollow tube called a *proboscis* (pro-BOSS-sis). They use this tube to reach deep into flowers where the nectar is located. When the proboscis is not being used, it stays coiled up underneath the butterfly's head.

SEE FOR YOURSELF

Would you like to try drinking like a butterfly? First, connect three or four drinking straws so that they become one long straw.

Fill a glass with fruit juice. Put one end of your giant straw into the glass and suck from the other end. Can you imagine drinking all your meals like this?

13

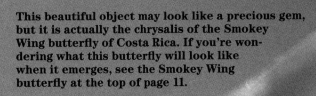

This beautiful object may look like a precious gem, but it is actually the chrysalis of the Smokey Wing butterfly of Costa Rica. If you're wondering what this butterfly will look like when it emerges, see the Smokey Wing butterfly at the top of page 11.

Butterflies and caterpillars are hunted by birds, lizards, monkeys, spiders, and many other animals. But as you will see below, they have some astonishing ways of staying alive. Most butterflies and caterpillars can blend in with their surroundings by looking like bark or leaves. Some can disguise themselves as bad-tasting insects that predators don't like to eat. And a few are actually poisonous to predators. Predators know which species these are, and they carefully avoid them.

Other butterflies use their bright colors to startle attackers. Some have spots on their wings that make them look scary to predators. And still others release a bad odor that drives predators away. All in all, butterflies and caterpillars need many ways to escape danger because predators lurk everywhere and can strike at any time!

The Indian Leaf butterfly is a master of disguise. As you can see at left, it is very colorful with its wings open. But when it closes them, below, it looks just like a leaf on a tree.

Birds are the chief predators of butterflies. Birds have more opportunities to catch butterflies than other animals because they can attack both in the air and on the ground.

Some butterflies, like the blue Morpho above, use their shiny wings to startle their predators. Called *flash coloration* (KUHL-uh-RAY-shun), this sudden, shimmering color startles the predator long enough for the butterfly to get away.

Some butterflies, like the one at right, are mildly poisonous. When a predator eats one, it usually gets sick. After that, it will remember not to eat this kind of butterfly again. Poisonous butterflies often have distinct colors and patterns, so they are easy to recognize.

POISONOUS ATROPHANEURA SWALLOWTAIL

POISONOUS SMOKEY WING BUTTERFLY

Some butterflies scare predators away by copying the appearance of poisonous species. This type of defense is called *mimicry* (MIM-ick-ree). Below are two butterflies and a moth that mimic the poisonous Smokey Wing butterfly of South America. Can you tell them apart?

NONPOISONOUS BUTTERFLIES

NONPOISONOUS MOTH

Long tails are used by some butterflies to fool predators. By rubbing its hind legs together, this Hairstreak butterfly can make its tails look like antennae. Birds and other predators then nip at the tails instead of at the butterfly's head.

The eyespots on the wings of this Owl butterfly from South America look like the eyes of an owl. And when it flaps its wings, the "eyes" look like they're blinking. This can scare away birds and other small animals that are afraid of owls.

Many caterpillars have eyespots on their skin that make them look like snakes. Some swallowtail caterpillars can even rear up at attackers to make themselves look more threatening!

Swallowtail caterpillars have the ultimate secret weapon — a Y-shaped fork in their heads called an *osmeterium* (OSS-meh-TAIR-ee-um). This fork releases an unpleasant odor that sends predators scrambling. And if the smell doesn't frighten them, the bright orange color usually does!

Some caterpillars disguise themselves by looking like bird droppings — something no predator wants to eat.

Monarch butterflies travel, or *migrate* (MY-grate), thousands of miles each year. Huge swarms of these butterflies leave their northern homes in fall, and head south for the winter. Then in spring, they fly north again to their original breeding grounds.

Many species of butterflies migrate to escape cold weather. But only the Monarch butterfly of North America makes a *true* migration — flying south and north again in the same year, *every* year. Some populations of Monarchs travel as far as 4,000 miles round-trip (6,436 kilometers)!

What makes this migration even more amazing is that no single butterfly completes the entire round-trip. The ones that begin the journey lay eggs and die along the way. Then their offspring take up the journey and find their way to the same places — even to the same trees — that their ancestors have been visiting for years! How they manage this is still a mystery to scientists.

Monarchs begin their journey before the autumn chill. Those living *east of the Rocky Mountains* fly the farthest—over 2,000 miles (3,218 kilometers) to Central Mexico! Those living *west of the Rockies* migrate about 1,000 miles (1,609 kilometers) to the California coast.

ROCKY MOUNTAINS

Eastern Monarchs travel in swarms to the plains of Mexico. After several thousand have gathered, they fly high into the mountains. Every year, they stop to rest on the same fir trees.

Some scientists think that migrating Monarchs have a built-in compass to point them in the right direction. Others believe that Monarchs simply navigate by using the sun.

Monarchs can migrate to Mexico in 2 months or less, depending on the weather. Even though they have only a 4-inch wingspan, Monarchs can travel over 1,000 miles (1,609 kilometers) in just a few days! And they even arrive *five times fatter* than when they left! That's because they feed on nectar along the way. And their coasting and gliding saves energy.

How can an animal as tiny as a butterfly migrate so many thousands of miles? Scientists have discovered that one way Monarchs do this is by hitching rides on winds, storms, and *even hurricanes* heading south! They glide on the wind currents, which carry them more than 7,000 feet (2,134 meters) above sea level. Airline pilots have reported seeing Monarchs as high as 29,000 feet (8,839 meters)!

About *200 million* Monarch butterflies spend their winter in a forest near Mexico City. Scientists estimate that there are as many as 10 million butterflies per acre in this forest! At times, the trees are literally covered with Monarchs.

The farther south they go, the choosier Monarchs become about the winds they ride. They prefer winds that are going toward their southern resting ground.

Scientists tag Monarchs to study them. This is a delicate operation. First, a small area at the top of the wing is gently brushed with the fingertips to clear it of scales. Then a tiny piece of adhesive paper is attached to the wing.

It wasn't until the mid-1970s that scientists discovered *where* all the millions of eastern Monarchs were gathering in Mexico. Scientists now capture, weigh, tag, and release both eastern and western Monarchs to learn more about their remarkable migration.

EIGHTY-EIGHT BUTTERFLY
(South America)

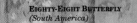

Thousands of butterfly species have become extinct in the last 50 years, most of them in the tropics. On these pages, you can see some of the most stunning and colorful of the living tropical species — from the dazzling Giant Blue Hercules with its shimmering blue wings to the spectacular Birdwings and Swallowtails.

TROPICAL SKIPPER
(Africa)

AFRICAN GIANT SWALLOWTAIL
(Africa)

FORMOSISSIMA BUTTERFLY
(South America)

GREAT BLUE HAIRSTREAK
(Ecuador)

BANANA EATER
(New Guinea)

CHIMAERA BIRDWING
(Papua New Guinea)

Tropical rainforests have more kinds of butterflies than any other region in the world. More than 10,000 species can be found in South America and Central America alone. When you compare that to the 89 species of butterflies in the whole state of Virginia, you can see why the tropics are so amazing!

Rainforests are perfect for butterflies. That's because their warm, damp climates are ideal for flowering plants to grow. And wherever plants are flowering, butterflies will be flitting about close by.

Unfortunately, these magical rainforests are in danger. People are clearing huge areas of forest to sell the timber or to make farms. And as the forests are wiped out, so are many of the plants and animals in them. Sadly, the beautiful tropical species are the most endangered of all butterflies.

THOAS SWALLOWTAIL
(South and Central America)

Every minute, an area of rainforest as large as 40 to 50 football fields is disappearing. Since *half of all animal and plant species in the world live in the tropics,* we stand to lose far more than we could possibly gain from cutting down these forests. Many beautiful butterflies will be lost forever.

PRIAMUS BIRDWING
(New Guinea)

Some countries like Taiwan have made butterfly collecting into a major industry. Although the Taiwanese export 15 million specimens a year, there is no decline in the butterfly population. Why? Because most of the butterflies are collected *after* they have laid their eggs.

MALAY LACEWING
(Malaysia)

GIANT BLUE HERCULES
(Papua New Guinea)

HELICONIUS BUTTERFLY
(South America)

AGRIAS BUTTERFLY
(Brazil)

Brazil, New Guinea, and other tropical countries sell hundreds of millions of butterflies to collectors each year. Fortunately, many of these specimens are raised on butterfly farms instead of being collected from the wild. More and more people are beginning to realize that butterfly farms, like the one above, can help save many species of butterflies.

HOMERUS SWALLOWTAIL
(Jamaica)

The largest butterfly collection in the world is at the London Museum of Natural History, with over 2 million specimens. But smaller butterfly collections, like the one at left, can be found in shops and museums all over the world. Collections such as these help scientists identify and better understand butterflies.

21

BUTTERFLIES ACTIVITIES

Don't flutter by these fun activities without trying them. Use what you have learned to complete the butterfly exercises on these two pages.

Picture Poetry

Read the picture poems below. Then try writing your own picture poem using words about butterflies. Arrange the words in the shape of a caterpillar or butterfly.

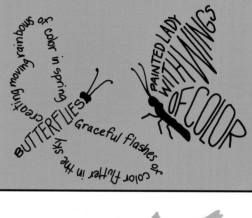

Build A Butterfly Farm

You can build a butterfly farm and watch caterpillars change into butterflies. You will need: *a large box, a hammer, a nail, a jar with a lid, scissors, tape, a sheet of clear plastic (try to recycle a clear plastic bag).*

1. Ask an adult to help you poke several small holes in the box so that the caterpillars can breathe. Then have the adult make four large holes in the lid of the jar. Fill the jar with water and replace the lid.

2. Collect some caterpillars and the plants they are on. Stick the stems of the plants through the holes in the jar lid. The stems should be long enough so that the plants will stay in the water. Place the jar inside the box.

3. Cut the sheet of clear plastic so that it is large enough to cover the open side of the box. Tape it over the ends of the box so that the caterpillars can't get out, but you can see in.

4. Watch the caterpillars grow each day. Make sure they always have enough food.

In time, each caterpillar will change into a chrysalis. This may take anywhere from a few days to several weeks. As soon as the butterflies emerge, remove the clear plastic. Watch but do not touch, as they dry themselves and fly away.

Butterfly Art

Make a colorful butterfly of your own. You will need: *colored tissue paper, scissors, black construction paper, a paintbrush, liquid starch or very thin white glue (mix equal amounts of water and white glue), waxed paper.*

1. Cut the tissue paper into about 20 to 30 1-inch (2.5 centimeter) squares. Use many different colors.

2. Fold a piece of black construction paper in half. Then fold it in half again. Next, trace the shape shown at left onto your folded paper. Make sure the shape begins and ends on a fold. Cut on the line you have drawn.

3. Make several cuts of different shapes in the folded piece of black paper. Then, open it up and look at your lacy butterfly.

4. Place your butterfly on a piece of waxed paper. Use a paintbrush to spread starch or thin white glue over one side of it. Next, put squares of tissue paper all over it. Make sure that all the cutout areas are covered by tissue. Then put a final coat of starch or glue over the whole butterfly.

5. When your design is dry, lift it off the waxed paper, tape it to a window, and let sunlight shine through the beautiful colo

The Code of the Butterflies

The letters in the three grids form a secret code. Each letter in the alphabet is represented by a special symbol. For example, A = □ and M = ⊡. Use the secret code to discover each of the six mystery butterfly words. On a piece of paper, write the letter that goes with each symbol.

A	B	C
D	E	F
G	H	I

J	K	L
M	N	O
P	Q	R

	S	T	U	
	V	W	X	
	Y	Z		

1.
2.
3.
4.
5.
6.

Caterpillar Cafe

Open a caterpillar and butterfly restaurant! You will need: *a garden pot, potting soil, seeds.*

Choose seeds from the menus below. All of these seeds will grow into plants that are favorite foods of caterpillars and butterflies. Caterpillars will munch on the leaves, while butterflies will flock to the flowers.

Place the potting soil in the garden pot. Add water to soak the soil. Plant the seeds according to the directions on the seed packages.

Be sure to water the plants when they sprout, but not too much. Water them again each time the soil feels dry. Soon your garden will be full of color and activity.

BUTTERFLY MENU
alfalfa
butterfly weed
catnip
common rue
dill
French marigold
golden rod
lavender
parsley
sage
thyme

CATERPILLAR MENU
alfalfa
butterfly weed
cabbage
common rue
dill
parsley
red clover

Index